Blessed are the
DIFFERENT

Blessed are the DIFFERENT

Biblical Answers for Human Questions

SEANA REAVIS

WESTBOW
P R E S S®
A DIVISION OF THOMAS NELSON
& ZONDERVAN

Cover art by Tammy Lashey and Nichole Womack

WestBow Press books may be ordered through booksellers or by contacting:

WestBow Press
A Division of Thomas Nelson & Zondervan
1663 Liberty Drive
Bloomington, IN 47403
www.westbowpress.com
1 (866) 928-1240

ISBN: 978-1-4908-9858-2 (sc)
ISBN: 978-1-4908-9859-9 (e)

Print information available on the last page.

WestBow Press rev. date: 03/03/2016

"If you truly believe that God is sovereign, then there is no such thing as deformity."

Tom Buck, Senior Pastor,
First Baptist Church of Lindale, TX.

"I don't have a disability. I have a platform to share my story, which is that I am blessed."

David Ring, Evangelist

CONTENTS

OUR STORY

Shepherd Morris Reavis calmly came into the world at 5:10pm on Tuesday, December 6, 2011. I say calmly because by his quiet demeanor at birth, you would never suspect that he was in any particular rush to arrive. Yet despite our expected weekly schedule, Shepherd willfully joined me and my husband, Josh, in person a month before his due date. While his cool persistence was cute at the time, it may be something that will come in handy, so to speak, throughout his life. That Tuesday afternoon, our baby slept smugly content in our arms, innocently unaware that he had just been born not only rather early, but also rather different.

This is a Bible study book especially for parents or caregivers of children with special needs. Family and friends may find it helpful as well, though it is written from one parent to another. I am not a writer. I am a wife and a mom who learned during my very first pregnancy that the child I carried was different, and I honestly struggled with accepting and appreciating that. I wish I could say that I felt honored from the moment we discovered the uniqueness of our child, but that would not be true. My husband's reaction was joy. *My* reaction was pure shock that left my heart heavy with questions and worry, all hidden behind an outward smile. I had been a Christian since age fourteen but upon revelation that God made my child with one hand instead of two, my response was anything but faithful. That struggle is the primary reason for this Bible devotional. I know I am not the only parent to battle with the reality of having a different child, and there are likely other parents, grandparents, and extended family who experience difficulty in embracing this particular blessing. Thankfully my struggle did not last long and the moment our son was born, my husband and I were *both* elated!

Yet how did I get there? What transformed a heart of cynicism into a heart of peace? It was the Word of God, and a lot of it. That is the foundation of this devotional. It has parts of my personal experience along with some wisdom from family and friends, but it is primarily a study of Scripture as it relates to special needs families. I wish I could have had a quick reference guide of Scripture verses that directly applied to the feelings I experienced at that sensitive time. Instead, I combed the Bible with my questions and God poured out His answers.

The news that your child is different can be acutely stressful, so while the book is set up as a devotional guide – designed in a short question and answer format - that can be completed in a matter of days, some may be able to digest more or less at a time. It has been kept as concise as possible because if you are expecting a child or you are already a parent, you have extremely limited time. My desire is that your heart and mind be filled with the truth and promises of our Creator God, with His words answering your deepest questions and giving you hope so that the grieving can end and the enjoyment of your child can be all that remains!

What I mean by "different"

… None like you has been before you and none like you shall arise after you.

1 KINGS 3:12 ESV

It is a well-known, scientific fact that every human being is inherently different from another. Almighty God is so amazingly creative that of all the billions of people that have ever existed, or are yet to exist, no two humans are ever exactly alike! Consequently it is true that every single child is different and special as an individual masterpiece. The terms "different, special needs, or unique" in *this* book are referring to children who have a noticeable or evident quality that distinguishes them from the expected norm. Every child is unique, but some differences are more visible or detectable. For example, my son was born with Left Transverse Terminal Limb Reduction Defect, an elaborate medical term to describe having no left hand. Your child's difference may be physical, cognitive, emotional, social, or any related diagnosis. It may have presented at birth, be a condition revealed later in childhood, or be the outcome of illness or injury. "Different" may also include that your family is composed of racial diversity and/or adopted members.

In this book, the terms "parents" and "your child" are used as generalizations to keep semantics simple and are not meant to exclude anyone. The Bible verses listed in each section are translated either in English Standard Version (ESV), New American Standard Bible (NASB), or New International Version (NIV), depending on which adaptation delivers the message with simplest clarity.

How did this happen?

For You formed my inward parts; You wove me in my mother's womb.

I will give thanks to You, for I am fearfully and wonderfully made;

Wonderful are Your works, and my soul knows it very well.

My frame was not hidden from You, when I was made in secret,

And skillfully wrought in the depths of the earth;
                                   PSALM 139:13-16 NASB

Before I formed you in the womb I knew you.
                                   JEREMIAH 1:5 NASB

When all of the tests were done, it was determined that Shepherd did not have a left hand simply because the blood vessels that normally travel down the arm to form into a hand and fingers just stopped and ended at his wrist instead. The doctors told us it was an unpredictable accident that occurs in approximately 1 out of every 6,900 babies, at about the 8th week of pregnancy. While it is understood that life comes into being through the process of biological conception, the Bible gives several much needed reminders that it is ultimately God who creates human souls and the bodies that house them.

The first truth in which parents absolutely must have confidence is this: your child is different *by design*. The Bible says in Psalm 139 that God formed your child in the womb. The words "wove" and "skillfully wrought" convey how intricate the details of your child's characteristics are. God's foreknowledge of your child is verified by the psalmist's words that "my frame was not hidden from you" and God's own verbal declaration in Jeremiah 1:5. In fact, since the Bible said we are made "in secret", it is certain that God knew our children long before *we* ever knew of them. It is natural for people to wonder and imagine what their future children may look like or which gender they will be. I am Korean and Josh is Caucasian so during our first six years of marriage we pondered over whose features would be more pronounced in the kids we would hopefully have one day. I always said I wanted them to at least have Josh's dimples and he would say he wished for them to have my eyes, which I would disagree with. We figured that our future children would all have dark hair. I really hoped they would have Josh's height yet my skin tone so that I would not have to deal with constant sunburn during our long Florida summers. Even though I had read Jeremiah 1:5 before, it never crossed my mind during those 6 years that before my son was even formed, while we could simply guess, God Himself knew Shepherd and already knew when and how He would make him.

God's foresight of your child includes any and every unique trait of their physical form. It is common for special needs children to undergo specific health evaluations that aim to identify a cause or risk factors of their difference. Perhaps you received a hereditary review concluding that your genetic history may have contributed to a diagnosis of your child. Another situation could be that clinicians determined that your age might have put your child at risk. Without disrespecting the profits of modern medical interpretation, it is valuable to remember that God is not controlled by scientific parameters, and He never has been. God knows all about your family history. God knew exactly how old you were when He formed your baby, just as He knew how old Sarah (Genesis 18:10-11) and Elizabeth (Luke 1:13,18) were when He formed each of theirs. God never makes a mistake, even if professionals may label a cause or classify a difference as a "fluke". I hope that you too will have faith that your child was indeed "fearfully and wonderfully made" (Psalm 139:14 ESV).

Where was God?

The Lord looks from heaven; He sees all the sons of men;

PSALM 33:13 NASB

The Lord is near.

PHILIPPIANS 4:5 NASB

And there is no creature hidden from His sight, but all things are open and laid bare to the eyes of Him with whom we have to do.

HEBREWS 4:13 NASB

The eyes of the Lord are in every place, watching the evil and the good.

PROVERBS 15:3 NASB

Does He care about the stress we have experienced?

Cast all your anxiety on Him because He cares for you.

1 PETER 5:7 NIV

Why did He let this happen?

> *I have chosen you and not rejected you.*
> ISAIAH 41:9 NASB

> *For I know the plans I have for you, declares the Lord, plans for welfare and not for evil, to give you a future and a hope.*
> JEREMIAH 29:11 ESV

> *And we know that God causes all things to work together for good to those who love God, to those who are called according to His purpose.*
> ROMANS 8:28 NASB

The truth that God forms children in the womb may be easier to acknowledge when a child's difference appears from birth or infancy. When your child's difference occurs as a result of an illness, injury, or trauma – when your child wasn't *born* different but *becomes* different – the question of "Where was God?" instinctively arises. Perhaps your child developed normally during pregnancy but then endured a distressed labor, or encountered an injury later in infancy or childhood. While this is a devastating experience that I have only seen and have not directly experienced, I hope that this book will point a parent in nearly any circumstance to the words of an omnipresent and sovereign God. I cannot provide any opinions concerning legal actions or relations with accountable parties, but would love to encourage you in the fact that the Bible assures us of God's love and mindfulness, even in the midst of our crisis. The promise we have from the Bible is threefold: God knows, God sees, and God cares about everyone. There is the temptation to assume that maybe international politics or the latest issue in the news took priority of God's attention at the hour your child was in need, but Hebrews 4:13 affirms to us that God was not distracted nor did He forget and abandon the safety of your child. Whatever the event, your family was never overlooked and your child's difference is not the result of an oversight on God's part. Moreover, Jeremiah 29:11 declares that God has a plan for his or her life, one that is not full of suffering and heartache, but one that includes a future and a hope!

It is my true belief that even in near fatal incidences that result in agonizing wounds, God ultimately preserved your child's life to have a special place in this world. As I have not personally walked the journey of having a child affected by a traumatic event, my friends Brent and Tricia have graciously shared their family's unforeseen experience.

"Our son, Bronson, was born on July 24, 2007. This day was the best and worst day of our lives. Bronson was a perfectly healthy baby until the day of his birth. Bronson suffered a severe brain injury the day that he was born due to oxygen depravation. The labor was long and strenuous. At one point his heart rate was lost for an entire hour. A C-section was requested, but denied for various reasons. Bronson was born lifeless and the NICU staff had to resuscitate him on two separate occasions to keep him alive. His life is indeed a miracle and what's even more miraculous is the way the Lord continues to use our son's joy for life on a daily basis for His glory and honor. Bronson is now a pleasant six-year-old young man. His diagnosis leaves him wheelchair bound with many uphill battles to conquer each and

every day, but through it all he continues to smile! This joy of his is a continuous reminder to us of how grateful we are for all the things in life that are so easy to take for granted. His diagnosis list is rather lengthy as is expected considering the severity of the brain injury. A few of the critical ones consist of cerebral palsy, epilepsy, cortical vision impairment, microcephaly, and dysautonomia. He has a feeding tube, appendicostomy and a suprapubic cystostomy. His heart rate and oxygen levels are monitored around the clock. He is on the ketogenic diet to control his seizures and we have to rescue him from autonomic storms (dysautonomia) approximately four times a day. His care can be very overwhelming and most doctors do not know what to do with him to be quite frank. We do the best we can to manage his daily needs and maintain him as much as possible to provide him the best day we can possibly offer him. The truth though is that he offers us so much more and we are so grateful to God for the blessing it is to be his parents.

We were both saved at young ages and have loved the Lord all of our lives. After Bronson's birth we were so confused. We didn't understand how God could let this happen to our precious baby. We were very angry to say the least. We were angry at the situation and angry with the Lord. We have been taught our whole lives that God is a God of miracles, and He is. We constantly prayed on hands and knees that the Lord would work a miracle in the life of our child. We prayed that Bronson would be healthy and whole when he left the NICU. Then we received the MRI results of his brain injury and we couldn't understand why the Lord didn't intervene on the behalf of our baby. There have been so many times since that day in the NICU that we have watched Bronson suffer and asked ourselves, 'Where are you Lord?' We have learned a big truth in these past six years. We have learned that sometimes the Lord says yes, sometimes He says no, and sometimes He says wait. We have learned to trust Him even when we can barely hear His voice through the pouring rain. We have learned to live with an eternal perspective every single day, knowing that one day Bronson will walk and talk in eternity. This world is not our home and this life is but a vapor.

The Lord really used this verse in our lives to help us understand how to look at our situation with Bronson from an eternal perspective. John 9:1-3 states, "As He was passing by, He saw a man blind from birth. His disciples questioned Him: 'Rabbi, who sinned, this man or his parents, that he was born blind? Neither this man nor his parents sinned' Jesus answered. <u>'This came about so that God's works might be displayed in him.</u>" This verse was life changing for us! Yes, the Lord allowed this but it's because He wanted to use our son in a mighty way so that the Lord's works will be displayed in Bronson! He chose our son to do this and He chose our family. We have since realized and truly have wrapped our hearts around the truth that the Lord sees the big picture and we cannot. Because of this the anger has vanished and our trust has been placed in the omniscience of our Heavenly Father. The Lord has a special purpose for every single person including our sweet Bronson. Yes, the Lord could have stopped Bronson's brain injury from happening but there is a reason He did not. We may never know what that reason is, but we can say that we know the Lord has a special purpose for it. We've come to a realization that there will always be special needs children in this world and the Lord decides who will be blessed with the privilege of taking care of one.

The Lord has taught us so many things these past six years and we can stand here today and say that being Bronson's parents is truly a blessing. We find it such a precious treasure to be the parents of a special needs child. We would have never learned the things we have without Bronson being in our lives. We see the world through new eyes and we are so grateful God choose us for this journey. Bronson is a sweet little boy with a contagious smile. He lights up our world, we would never change him, and he is our hero."

~ Brent and Tricia Roth

Why me? Why my child?

*To one He gave five talents, to another, two, and
to another, one, each according to his own ability;*
MATTHEW 25:15 NASB

*For as the heavens are higher than the earth,
So are My ways higher than your ways and My
thoughts than your thoughts.*
ISAIAH 55:9 NASB

*before you were born I consecrated you; I appointed
you a prophet to the nations.*
JEREMIAH 1:5 ESV

*… in Your book were written, every one of them,
the days that were formed for me,
when as yet there was none of them.*
PSALM 139:16 ESV

I remember asking God why He wanted my child to suffer,
imagining an innocent baby subjected to pitiful stares and
constant physical challenges. All I could see was a little boy
fumbling through a hard life with only one hand. Oddly
enough, my eyes were fixated on the one thing that wasn't
there rather than all the other parts that he *did* have. I
cannot presume to answer why God made my child or

your child different because the Bible says His ways are infinitely higher than our ways (Isaiah 55:9). Many times I have to caution myself to beware of the expectation that I am entitled to receive an explanation anytime God chooses to act in my life. Even though we may not see the whole picture from start to finish, God has eternal vision and He knew all the days of our children's lives before they ever took their first breath! God told Jeremiah, "before you were born I consecrated you; I appointed you a prophet to the nations." (Jeremiah 1:5 ESV). The psalmist David praised God saying, "Your eyes saw my unformed substance; in your book were written, every one of them, the days that were formed for me, when as yet there was none of them." (Psalm 139:16 ESV). Just as God had a vision to anoint Jeremiah as a prophet and ordain David as a king, God created my child and your child for a purpose that He already foreknew before He even formed them.

Accepting that God is sovereign over your child's form, and even that their difference is for a purpose, is much easier than also appreciating it. Our tendency is to merely accept it as if to be one's cross to bear or thorn in the side that God chose to put in our lives to keep us humble. Yet the Bible says, "And we know that God causes all things to work together for good to those who love God, to those who are called according to *His* purpose." (Romans 8:28 NASB). I had to move beyond simply accepting God's will for Shepherd's life to really trusting that God's will for his life was for his *good*, that there was not only a purpose for his form but that it was a *good* purpose. Above what I think is good for my son, I want what God thinks is good for my son. If that means him being different, then not only do I accept it, but I am thankful for it.

God has a master plan and He has made a place in it for your family to have a part. God gave you and your child to each other. Some have said that, "God gives special children to special parents", and I actually agree with that statement to a degree. I believe that God gives parents of special children an extraordinary responsibility with the choice to step up to it or not. As much as it was God's will to give your child to you, it was His will to give you to your child as his or her parent. On occasion I have struggled because I know that I am not worthy to be the mother of such a special child as Shepherd. I have met women who are serenely patient and nurturing, and I never considered myself to be either of those things. I wondered if my son would have been better suited to have a mother who was the epitome of composed wisdom and boundless tranquility, not a loud talker with tiger mother tendencies. Despite how I feel or think, God said that His thoughts and ways are higher than mine. In Matthew 25:15 He gave each servant according to his ability. God had plans for you and your child, and it included you both being in each other's lives. You may feel trepidation about the task of parenting a child with special needs or you may doubt that you are the right choice as his or her parent but God will not call you to something that He will not equip you for. Remember, God even consecrated Jeremiah for his duty before birth. Appreciate what God has done in your family's life and rise with confidence to the rewarding challenge of parenting your fearfully and wonderfully made child!

Two things often happen when you become a special needs parent. The first is that you become nearly an expert of knowledge in the area of your child's difference. Parents can go from being completely unfamiliar with a particular diagnosis to having the most specialized comprehension in almost no time. Secondly, you meet and share understanding with fellow parents. In my conversations with other parents, the most common shared experiences have been in the questions we have asked God and ourselves when we first learned of our child's difference. Regardless of the type of difference, nearly all parents at first wonder the same thing, "Why?". My friend Pam has a daughter whose difference is unlike that of my son's, but she spoke of her own experience with that same question and the blessing of being chosen to parent a special child.

"'Why me? Why my child?' I asked myself those questions many times after learning my sweet baby would have Down Syndrome... Although we were saddened at the news, God wasn't surprised. He knew all along.

We relied heavily on Matthew 25:15, 'To one He gave five talents, to another two, and to another one, each according to his ability', and Psalms 139:13-16 'For you formed my inward parts; you knitted me together in my mother's womb. I praise you, for I am fearfully and wonderfully made. Wonderful are your works; my soul knows it very well. My frame was not hidden from you, when I was being made in secret, intricately woven in the depths of the earth. Your eyes saw my unformed substance; in your book were written, every one of them, the days that were formed for me, when as yet there was none of them.'

Parenthood has brought us some of our greatest challenges. It's also brought moments of sheer joy! We know God has a purpose for our little girl. She's Heaven sent. On July 2nd, we got to meet our sweet little girl – 5 weeks earlier than expected and oh, the joy felt at holding her for the first time – she looked into my eyes as if to say – 'JUST LOVE ME and everything will be ok'. She's not a mistake. She's not a devastating tragedy. She is absolutely perfect just the way the good Lord made her. We are so proud to be the parents of a child with an extra chromosome. God has opened our eyes to the needs of others. We've made some new friends that we probably would not have met had we not been blessed with our little girl and we have a new passion and a love for children that are 'differently-abled.'"

~Pam Harvey

DID I CAUSE THIS OR AM I BEING PUNISHED FOR SOMETHING?

As He passed by, He saw a man blind from birth. And His disciples asked Him, "Rabbi, who sinned, this man or his parents, that he would be born blind?"

Jesus answered, "It was not that this man sinned, or his parents; but that the works of God might be displayed in him."

JOHN 9:1-3 ESV

The question of whether you could have done anything to prevent your child's difference is one that plagues most parents at some point. If the two main personalities are Type A and Type B, I suppose I would have to relax a little to at least fall into the Type A category. Truly, even a Type A personality would probably consider me to be somewhat intense. In keeping with my nature, I approached my pregnancy with zeal, as if imagining that I was aiming for a perfect score on a science project. By the time it was confirmed that we were expecting, I had already been taking prenatal vitamins for two months. Check! And I never missed a single daily dose.

Check! I slept approximately 8 (and more!) hours nightly. Check! I consumed approximately 300 extra calories each day and ate a nutritious all natural diet that included only fully cooked meats and pasteurized dairy. Check! I exercised regularly yet cautiously. Check! My husband and I read all of the best-rated books and attended each hospital class on labor, infant CPR, and baby proofing our house. Check Check Check! As you may imagine, at 24 weeks pregnant I skipped into the ultrasound room practically expecting my A+ baby to turn towards the monitor and give me a thumbs up. In reality, the sonographer spent about half an hour running the equipment over every angle while I happily gazed at the blurry grey and white image rolling around on the screen. I was oblivious to the passing time, and the serious look on the woman's face, as I now know that she was not looking for a thumbs up but rather an entire left hand. Once the sentences, "I don't see anything beyond your baby's left forearm" and "so I believe he does not have a hand there" sunk in, my mind spun in confusion. How could he be missing a hand?! I did everything right to promote him growing without any complications so how could this be happening? It bewildered me that I had put in every good effort to not have the result I expected. Then when the prenatal specialist insisted that she had seen limb differences occur in both the healthiest and unhealthiest pregnancies, I pondered, "If it can't be my physical behaviors, then where did I misstep spiritually that God would do this? Why else would He allow this if not to teach me a lesson because of something I did to displease Him?"

I actually did not remember John 9:1-3 myself, but a dear friend shared it with me as we talked on the phone soon after my sonogram. She had just studied that passage of Scripture at her church the weekend before, and I do not believe it was a coincidence that she was then able to encourage me with it. The answer to my question was so clear: God was not punishing me, or my child. Of course I understand that situations do occur in which damaging or irresponsible behaviors during pregnancy cause severe effects. However, if your actions have not been neglectful or sinful, please allow the passage to bring your heart some relief! If you too can cry out like the author of Psalm 139:23, "Search me, O God, and know my heart! Try me and know my thoughts! And see if there be any grievous way in me" (ESV), then I hope that you will resist the self-inflicted pain of blaming yourself.

EVEN IF I DON'T BLAME MYSELF, WILL OTHERS BLAME ME?

If we evaluate our circumstances based one the reactions of people around us, then we are in danger of valuing man's opinions over God's thoughts. Is man always correct? No. Is God always correct? Thankfully, yes! It is occasionally awkward in grocery lines or parks when strangers look at Shepherd and then glance at me, as I can see their eyes trace over me trying to quickly pick up on any clues that might lead to understanding how this sweet little boy ended up with only one hand. I've seen the wheels turning behind the stares and heard the reasoning behind the loud whispers of possible drug use or poor prenatal care. You learn to get over what strangers think pretty quickly but it can be especially disheartening when so-called fellow believers have a similar reaction.

Going back to John 9:2, we see that Christ's own disciples assumed that there may have been a parent who sinned and that the man's blindness must have been God's retribution. Thus it should not be surprising that some of Christ's followers today, like those in the passage, might also make the same mistaken assumption. It is almost human instinct to look for a fault, whether we claim to follow Jesus or not. Yet the Lord challenged their flawed theory. The man's blindness was not a punishment for sin, but in fact, God had a miracle planned for his life! The man was different *by design* and that difference put him in front of the Lord Jesus, who would do a great work in and through his life!

All moms can agree and usually laugh in hindsight about the careless or insensitive remarks that a pregnant woman receives at a vulnerable time. There you are, feeling like a circus elephant with feet swelling out of your shoes and a lady who should totally know better makes a comment about how big you look... or teasingly asks you how many babies you are carrying. Yet I assure you from experience, that is nothing compared to a comment (or a comment disguised as a question) implicating you as the cause of your child's "handicap". There may be only one or two things on earth that are more crushing to a mom-to-be than to insinuate that the child she carries is not only deformed, but that she is to blame. Jokes about my pregnant penguin waddle did little to mortify me, but my heart sank every single time someone stood right in front of me and implied that maybe I did not take the best care of my growing child that I loved so much. People are naturally curious. We don't *need* to know information about others, but we want to. Sometimes that leads us to ask questions of people that may quench our curiosity but unwittingly causes them hurt as well. People were certainly curious of Shepherd and asked a broad array of questions: if the doctors suspected that his hand didn't form because of exposure to any toxins (no), if my doctor knew I wore high heels during all three trimesters (yep), or if this type of abnormality was more common in Asians (not particularly).

I am so thankful that this story is in the Bible for us to see. It was such a comfort to me whenever I feared judgment or doubted myself. This passage can uplift you if you experience discouragement but please take heart and beware of suspecting a critical tone in every encounter. These verses are a great reassurance if such encounters occur but they may actually never, or they may be rare. Josh and I were so fortunate to have a great measure of support from family, friends, and our church. The reception from those close to us was what we knew to expect from people who truly knew us as a couple. Those around us who were Christ honoring, sensitive, and positive reacted in a Christ honoring, sensitive, and positive way. We seldom received a comment that was out of character or unexpected from individuals. There is the possibility of an occasional criticism, but take a moment to consider the source and remember this story in John 9:1-3, as well as any support that you have around you from people who have truly considerate words to offer.

Is this a trial?

Behold, children are a gift of the LORD,
The fruit of the womb is a reward.

Like arrows in the hand of a warrior,

So are the children of one's youth.

How blessed is the man whose quiver is full of them;

PSALM 127:3-5 NASB

And when Esau lifted up his eyes and saw the women and children,

he said, "Who are these with you?"

Jacob said, "The children whom God has graciously given your servant."

GENESIS 33:5 ESV

Consider it all joy, my brethren, when you encounter various trials, knowing that the testing of your faith produces endurance.

And let endurance have its perfect result, so that you may be perfect and complete, lacking in nothing.

But if any of you lacks wisdom, let him ask of God, who gives to all generously and without reproach, and it will be given to him.

JAMES 1: 2-5 NASB

Is this a trial? No, quite the opposite in fact. The Bible clearly states, "children are a gift from the Lord" that "God has graciously given". You may find yourself receiving Bible verses from well-meaning Christians seeking to encourage you through what they perceive to be a trial in your life, and that is very benevolent. However, a trial is defined as the testing of one's faith, and a child does not meet that description. That is not to say that there won't be actual trials while parenting a different child – there are significant trials while parenting in general, but the child *as an individual is not the trial itself.* Your child is a blessing - a living soul graciously given to you as a stewardship from God. When the "trials of various kinds" do come into the life of your family, God tells us to "count it all joy… for you know that the testing of your faith produces steadfastness. And let steadfastness have its full effect, that you may be perfect and complete, lacking in nothing." For the moments when you are overwhelmed with stress, or do not know what to say or how to react, the Bible continues with, "If any of you lacks wisdom, let him ask God, who gives generously to all without reproach, and it will be given to him."

EVEN THOUGH I BELIEVE THE BIBLE, WHY AM I STILL STRUGGLING?

Put on the whole armor of God, that you may be able to stand against the schemes of the devil. For we do not wrestle against flesh and blood, but against the rulers, against the authorities, against the cosmic powers over this present darkness, against the spiritual forces of evil in the heavenly places.

EPHESIANS 6:11-12 ESV

Be sober-minded; be watchful. Your adversary the devil prowls around like a roaring lion, seeking someone to devour.

1 PETER 5:8 ESV

The spirit indeed is willing, but the flesh is weak.
MATTHEW 26:41 ESV

The first few weeks following our Friday sonogram that revealed Shepherd's single hand were basically a blur. The news spread nearly instantly, reaching churches outside of our own and friends of friends of friends before the weekend was even finished. Within hours of our sonogram, we were met with a wave of people offering prayer, encouragement, shared experiences, and plenty of well-intentioned sympathy. As a Christian, preacher's wife, and Sunday school teacher I knew all of the righteous replies to the chief question of how we were handling things. I knew the Bible said that God was in control, all-knowing, and all-powerful. I knew the Bible said that God made children and that they are a blessing. I knew the Bible said that He loved all people and that He was good. I knew the Bible overflowed with words of His kindness, mercy, grace, hope, peace, strength, comfort, and faithfulness. I also knew that I questioned all of it during that stressful time. My questions were leading to doubts, and my doubts were escalating to resentment.

One night after the pressure in my heart had mounted for several days, I poured a glass of milk as it had been my custom to cap off each day with a serving of calcium for mommy and baby. As I sat at the table to finish my glass, my eyes caught a glimpse of the sonogram pictures that had been resting there since the week before. I picked one up and stared blankly at a clear image of two arms held out, with one significantly shorter than the other. At that moment I crumbled into tears and I spoke aloud what I consider to be one of my most regrettable statements. I held up the glass to my husband and angrily questioned, "What's the point of even drinking this milk?! It obviously doesn't matter how well I take care of the baby if God is just going to make him however He wants anyway!" At that point, Josh, who had been ever so patient throughout that last week of my depressed reclusiveness, sat beside me and decisively replied, "Stop Sarah. This is spiritual warfare and you have to fight!

Satan wants to you be mad at God and think He made a mistake, and to even think that something is wrong with our son and you have to fight back!" Sure enough, as rapidly as my mind had spiraled into frustration over the course of the week, so did it seem to rebound to clarity in an instant at my kitchen table. Of course this was a spiritual attack, and I was so embarrassed that I had fallen for the old trick of self-pity!

Commonly, Satan is viewed as solely the enemy of God, or as a figure of speech to represent general evil in the world. Recognizing him as an enemy of each individual - who actively schemes in people's daily lives - can be considered creepy or strange. If you were to bring up in casual conversation that you felt the devil was attacking an aspect of your life, there may be some awkward reactions. It can be uncomfortable to think of such a fearful character. Yet, 1 Peter 5:8 calls the devil *our* adversary as well, and Ephesians 6:11 urges us to be prepared to resist him. We see from these verses that while it is not ideal to become obsessed with the devil's agenda, it is not beneficial to dismiss the reality of his confrontations with our personal lives. John 8:44 identifies Satan as the father of lies, and he will subtly distort even the blessing of children and tempt you to view it as a curse. He wants you to believe that God forgot you, that your child is the result of an accident gone terribly wrong. John 10:10 calls Satan a thief who "comes only to steal, kill, and destroy". Know that what God meant for your good, Satan wants to turn into evil (Genesis 50:20a ESV). As grand as God's plans are for your life, Satan has his plans too. He wants you to think that your child is deformed. He wants you to resent and reject your child, and ultimately God Himself. When I realized this, that was the moment I snapped back to truth and I was furious that I was falling for lies.

The question of why we struggle to believe the Bible and not reject it in the hour of hardship applies to nearly any area of life, so it is no surprise that the answer is familiar. A believer in Christ is a new creation (2 Corinthians 5:17), a saved soul. However, that soul is still carried around in a body of flesh and bone. In our humanness, we wrestle with fear and doubt. In Matthew 26:41, Jesus said that even though the spirit is willing to resist temptation, our flesh is weak. The Bible clearly teaches in Ephesians 6:12 that spiritual warfare is very real, and it is not limited to only battles over salvation or heavy addictions. Satan will pick a fight anywhere in your life and he sees nothing as off limits, not even children.

If the battle of faith is raging on in your life, I have been there, and I urge you to fight back. Bitterness is a slippery slope and I could feel it pulling me down farther. I am thankful that my husband had the courage to walk right up to that dark place and kindly lead his wavering wife away from it. My first hard climb over an obstacle as a mother occurred before Shepherd was even born. It started with me asking God to forgive my blame, and by finishing my glass of milk.

WILL MY CHILD BE TEASED? HOW WILL I GIVE PROTECTION FROM HURT FEELINGS?

But the LORD said to Samuel, "Do not look at his appearance or at the height of his stature, because I have rejected him; for God sees not as man sees, for man looks at the outward appearance, but the LORD looks at the heart.

1 SAMUEL 16:7 NASB

Your hands made me and fashioned me;

Give me understanding, that I may learn Your commandments…

O may Your lovingkindness comfort me, according to Your word to Your servant.

PSALM 119:73, 76 NASB

I have to admit that I think my son is so handsome and complete that my heart breaks at the thought of him being the subject of a joke. It is such a low blow to make fun of something that a person obviously cannot control or change.

The cruelest part of it is sometimes the sheer availability of the joke. A visible difference is noticeable for everyone to observe. Less obvious qualities such as a person's neurotic tendencies or pitchy singing voice are not as easy of a target. When I think about a typical schoolyard, teasing is sadly common. Young children are curious, but school-aged kids can be harsh and everyone is aware of this.

Since Shepherd's appearance is so obviously different, it is tempting for me to fixate on the idea that he will be derided for his hand the most. Will your child be made fun of? Maybe, and maybe even for what you think they might be. But they could also be just as easily provoked for something else. Why? Frankly, because kids often make fun of other kids in general. You might even be able to recall being made fun of yourself, even if you weren't markedly different. Perchance you even made fun of someone else. I was made fun of in school for having tiny eyes, for being overweight, for not having a mom living with me. Regrettably, I myself made fun of others in school as well. Kids today are ridiculed for almost anything under the sun. They're poor, they're rich, they're skinny, they're heavy, they're tall, they're short, they're quiet, they're loud, they're ahead in class, they're behind in class, and so on. Is any of this right? Absolutely not, but unfortunately we live in a world where people are not always taught to respect or value others.

I do not have an entire conversation planned already, but I do intend to explain to Shepherd the meaning of 1 Samuel 16:7. By nature people look at the outside appearance. That can amount to simply describing someone physically or it can even apply as deep as only seeing a person's worth as a sum of external characteristics. God sent the prophet Samuel to anoint the next king of Israel and warned him against focusing on "his appearance or the height of his stature". God calls mankind out for our propensity to judge based on looks and teaches us a vital lesson about Himself: He is not as impressed with looks as we are. I plan to teach Shepherd that in Psalm 119:73, it says that God made and fashioned him, and that God said He looks to see what is in a person's heart. As in Psalm 119:76, my prayer of protection will be for God to give my son understanding and for His lovingkindness to comfort him not matter what adversity he may face.

WILL MY CHILD BE UPSET ABOUT BEING DIFFERENT?

Can a woman forget her nursing child, that she should have no compassion on the son of her womb? Even these may forget, yet I will not forget you. Behold, I have engraved you on the palms of My hands;

ISAIAH 49:15-16a ESV

It is the Lord who goes before you. He will be with you; He will not leave you or forsake you. Do not fear or be dismayed.

DEUTERONOMY 31:8 ESV

Do not fear, for I am with you;
Do not anxiously look about you, for I am your God.
I will strengthen you, surely I will help you,
Surely I will uphold you with My righteous right hand.

ISAIAH 41:10 NASB

For weeks I wrestled with the prospect of having a different child, alternating between feelings of disappointment and of shame over my disappointment. However, by my 7th month God had reassured me through His Word about what a blessing Shepherd was, and I had a renewed excitement about our soon-to-arrive baby boy. The only burden that seemed to linger was my concern that he would grow to one day resent his left arm. Josh and I believed that God created Shepherd just as he was, but would he believe that as well? Would he have a biblical view of the world and himself? Even if he was courageous and very comfortable with himself, would he still deal with discouragement? The thought of Shepherd experiencing resentment because of his God-given appearance haunted me as I felt him roll and kick beneath my heavy heart.

Everyone likely knows that you cannot determine or control your child's feelings. Even careful parental direction does not carry any promises of fruitful results. Ultimately, our children must decide for themselves to accept God's Word as truth. However, God did say that if we "train up a child in the way he should go, even when he is old he will not depart from it" (Proverbs 22:6 ESV). If we are faithful to sow God's word into the lives of our children, they are once and forevermore under the knowledge of it. Aside from teaching our children that they are wonderfully made, what else can we do? We can teach them about their true identity and about God's constant presence.

Identity versus Identification: How your child is *identified* is not necessarily their actual *identity*. If you had an appointment to meet my husband somewhere, I would tell you to be looking for a tall young man with dark hair and glasses. I would not tell you to keep your eyes open for a man who loves Jesus, is exceptionally patient, and is a homebody. His outward identifying features give no indication of his inward character. Similarly, Shep will often be identified in public as the boy with one hand. There is nothing wrong with that - his one handedness is wonderful - but he is so much more. What he looks like is not the core of his being. So while having a single hand will be an obvious way to identify him, it does not need to be what defines him. I will never introduce my children as "this is my adopted daughter Anna Rose" or "this is my single-handed son Shepherd". Neither should your child need to carry his or her difference around as a constant adjective preceding his or her identity.

God's constant presence: I know that I cannot control Shepherd's view of his self-worth. I also know that unlike God, I cannot be present at all places and times in his life, although sometimes I wish I could. Your child may have few or frequent struggles as a result of being different. You may not be there to rescue him or her from every uncomfortable situation but God promises in Isaiah 49, "I will not forget you. Behold, I have engraved you on the palms of my hands". He says not to be dismayed, that He will be with your child even when you are not. Deuteronomy 31:8 and Isaiah 41:10 guarantees that God will not forsake your child, and He will give strength and help in the difficult times.

HOW BIG/SMALL A DEAL SHOULD I MAKE OF THIS AS MY CHILD GROWS?

Love the Lord your God with all your heart and with all your soul and with all your strength. These commandments that I give you today are to be on your hearts. Impress them on your children. Talk about them when you sit at home and when you walk along the road, when you lie down and when you get up. Tie them as symbols on your hands and bind them on your foreheads. Write them on the doorframes of your houses and on your gates.

DEUTERONOMY 6:5-9 NIV

Train up a child in the way he should go, Even when he is old he will not depart from it.

PROVERBS 22:6 ESV

bring them up in the discipline and instruction of the Lord.

EPHESIANS 6:4 ESV

Both professionals and fellow parents have advised us that children learn to perceive their difference mainly by parental influence. If the parents view their children as disabled and treat them as limited, then the children will learn to esteem themselves at or below that standard. Likewise, most well-adapted and confident children have usually been educated about their individuality with nurture and edification. Children are very bright and sense negative attitudes, even despite a parent's words or actions. If you are not content with your child's difference, no matter what you may say aloud, they will probably internalize your true feelings. The perceptive awareness of a growing child challenges us as parents to decide here and now to accept our child as the blessing God intended. Still the question remains of how much attention we should give to the difference itself. For instance, should I ignore Shepherd's left arm completely and just expect him to do everything exactly as everyone else, or should I highlight his difference and constantly talk about it?

I understand that some special needs require a great amount of time, energy, cost, and work on a daily basis. There are some conditions that involve so much care that the simple day to day demands seem to center around your child's needs. Still, as a parent you may wonder how much focus should be given to your child's difference beyond meeting his or her basic developmental requirements. It is wonderful to celebrate your child's unique qualities, and in a world where scores of children live in belittling environments, I cannot say enough of how important I feel it is to applaud every milestone in your special child's life. With that being said, I have to remind myself that Shepherd's difference is not the most central thing about him, and that it is not what my every word should revolve around. In Deuteronomy, God tells parents that the most critical thing to emphasize in a child's life is to "love the Lord your God with all your heart and with all your soul and with all your strength". God said to teach these words diligently, to the point that they are the highest priority in conversation at home and everywhere else. Above what distinguishes your child as unique, we as parents are first called to elevate God's commands "when you sit at home and when you walk along the road, when you lie down and when you get up". It is what I have to remember to speak of the *most* within my family. In today's culture, parenting continues to evolve to resemble a lenient cheer squad whose main priority is to patrol and uphold a child's self esteem. The Bible tasks us as parents to model an appreciation of our self worth in light of God's love, and to give Him the highest place in our heart, soul, and mind. That is the biblical attitude that allows our children to develop a proper perspective of their difference and to understand their greatest purpose.

SINCE GOD MADE MY CHILD DIFFERENT, IS HE OR SHE MORE SPECIAL?

For God does not show favoritism.
ROMANS 2:11 NIV

Parents of uncommonly different children can sometimes land on two opposing ends of a spectrum in regards to this question - either believing that their child is less special and feeling depressed, or believing that their child is more special and feeling entitled. The scale range is far and wide: It's nothing/it's everything, it's what makes them disabled/it's what makes them better, it's the hardest part of them/it's the best part of them. An example of imbalance sometimes presents in the case of adopted children: Some are treated as second-rate compared to biological children whereas some are told they are more special because they were *chosen*, making biological children by comparison seem like accidental obligations. We even see examples of imbalances on both ends of the spectrum in Scripture.

> *"But the Lord said to Samuel, 'Do not look on his appearance or on the height of his stature, because*

I have rejected him. For the Lord sees not as man sees: man looks on the outward appearance, but the Lord looks on the heart.'" 1 SAMUEL 16:7 ESV

The context of this passage is that God sent the prophet Samuel to anoint the future king of Israel at a banquet where Jesse and his sons would be attending. Samuel was not initially aware of which son would be chosen, but God had cautioned him not to judge by outward appearances alone. After all seven of the present sons passed before Samuel, it was clear that God had not chosen any of them. The chosen one turned out to be the youngest son David, who was not at the banquet but was charged with tending the sheep. David should have been included at the banquet but in that culture at that time it was unheard of that the youngest child would be anointed for anything so honorable. In *your* culture at *this* time, how will you see your child? Even today, nations still exist where different children are devalued or considered cursed. Will you allow the current culture of the world to dictate the potential you see in your child or will you believe that God can do anything in his or her life? What a shame that Jesse missed it but there can be the mistake on the other end of the spectrum as well:

> *"Then the mother of the sons of Zebedee came to Jesus with her sons, bowing down and making a request of Him. And He said to her, 'What do you wish?' She said to Him, 'Command that in Your kingdom these two sons of mine may sit one on Your right and one on Your left.' But Jesus answered, 'You do not know what you are asking.'"*
> MATTHEW 20:20 NASB

It is natural for parents to feel that their child is the most special child in all the world. This is true for myself, as my child is the most special child in all the world to *me*. It is not right however, to claim that my child is more special to God than any other child that was created. Out of the twelve disciples, the mother of James and John behaved as if she believed her sons to be more important than the others and more important to Jesus. She boldly requested that they be given a higher place in God's kingdom. I do not want to ever dismiss my child as Jesse did, nor elevate him like the mother of James and John.

Balance of these two extremes lies in the awareness that God made *each* individual different yet *equally* special. I hope to view my child as Samuel's mother, Hannah (1 Samuel 1:27), or Moses' mother, Jochebed (Exodus 2:2). These two women prayed for their children, saw that they were special, and allowed their lives to be directed by the will of God. Being different does not equate to less of a human being or soul. Shepherd doesn't think or feel less, nor does he have less of a right to basic dignity or common courtesy. Conversely, he is not innately more important to God. Children are all different - either inwardly or outwardly – and will have variable experiences and opportunities in life, but they all share the same irreplaceable worth.

SINCE MY CHILD IS DIFFERENT, IS AN EXTRAORDINARY LIFE PROBABLE?

Now to Him who is able to do far more abundantly than all that we ask or think, according to the power at work within us, to Him be glory in the church and in Christ Jesus throughout all generations, forever and ever.

EPHESIANS 3:20-21 ESV

I can do all things through Him who strengthens me.

PHILIPPIANS 4:13 ESV

I am the vine; you are the branches. If you remain in Me and I in you, you will bear much fruit; apart from Me you can do nothing.

JOHN 15:5 NIV

I have a growing scrapbook of news articles headlining people with limb differences who have made great accomplishments. These pictures and stories of wounded veterans, athletes, professionals, and influential figures are meant to encourage Shepherd that his left arm is no reason to hold back in life.

The scrapbook is just to motivate him to never let his physical body be an excuse for not trying his best. Not every different child is destined to be the next celebrity role model, even if their difference does usually make them stand out more. We must also define what we characterize as extraordinary versus ordinary, what is success versus failure. Jesus once healed ten people and only one returned to Him. In that case while ten received a successful healing, only one made the successful life choice and returned to Jesus. That being said, Philippians 4:13 teaches us that we "can do all things through Him who strengthens" (ESV). There are many examples in the Bible of average people that God used to achieve incredible things. Moses was fearful of speaking in public, yet God used him to lead the nation of Israel out of Egyptian bondage. Esther was an orphaned girl that God used to save the minority Jewish people from genocide. Mary was a humble teenager who God called to give birth to the Savior of mankind. Jesus even used the five loaves of bread and two fish belonging to an unnamed boy to feed thousands of people. The most extraordinary thing about all of these people was their willingness to submit their lives to God.

Our children need to discover who God created them to be, whether or not that purpose is viewed as remarkable by the world. The passages in Ephesians, Philippians, and John all speak of the possibility of people living extraordinarily through the power of an extraordinary God. None of the passages emphasizes fame or the person themselves to be the focus. Above any extraordinary dream that we have for our children, the greatest of them all is to have the power of God in their lives. He will be able to do far more through them than anything we could ever ask or think.

How do I handle the attention?

You are the light of the world. A city set on a hill cannot be hidden. Nor do people light a lamp and put it under a basket, but on a stand, and it gives light to all in the house. In the same way, let your light shine before others, so that they may see your good works and give glory to your Father who is in heaven.

MATTHEW 5:14-16 ESV

Reality is your child will likely draw more attention from people and be more memorable to a stranger than the average person. This is a fact of life that has just as much potential to be daunting as it has potential to be beneficial. While stares or tactless questions can be irritating, attention comes in other ways than the occasional finger pointing. Often people are curious to understand not only the details surrounding your child's difference, but also how he carries himself. People look to see how the child and his or her family perceive the difference and how it affects their attitude or expectations about life. Basically, they want to see if you and your child are living below, at, or above circumstances that are widely perceived as difficult or unwanted. It is true that sometimes you will have more eyes on you because your family is different. You can resent or try to hide from this extra attention or you can turn it into an opportunity.

Jesus said, "A city set on a hill cannot be hidden" to illustrate how believers with the light of Christ stand out in a dark world. But just as a city set on a hill cannot be hidden, generally neither can distinctly different children and their families. As a baby, strangers' eyes were usually fixated on Shepherd's left arm. Even today, he is the king of double takes. When we are walking through a crowd, people glance, are hit with surprise, then quickly snap their heads back again. It is good to keep in mind that most of the attention is not ill willed at all but simply curiosity. Sometimes people even wanted to see Shepherd's arm when he was first born so that they could specifically point out how wonderful they thought it was that he was different. Young children are naturally curious and funnily enough, in public they will often ask the questions their accompanying adults would actually like to. A typical conversation between us and an innocently curious child usually goes like this:

"Hey, what happened to his hand?"

"He was born with one hand."

"Oh, does it hurt?"

"Not at all."

"Ok cool."

The fact that people take more notice of your child can also provide an occasion to relate with others and share a life-changing message of hope. God has an incredible way of connecting people. Practically everywhere you look people are bonding over shared hobbies, careers, friends, neighborhoods, and frequently, shared experiences. If you have experienced anything that another person has also been through, then you know that there is a unique sense of understanding. Even though the Bible never says that life will be easy everyday, Christians sometimes buy into the myth that because Jesus is our Savior and Lord, we should have a force field around us to protect us from any challenges. Yet a challenging experience may be the only thing that links you to someone who needs to hear about the love of God. Perhaps there is someone who chooses to live life without God but they listen to you speak of your spiritual devotion solely because you are also a parent of a child with special needs.

We, and I am certainly including myself, must remember that the Bible always points people to a relationship with God through Jesus Christ. We live in a fractured world where multitudes of people live without peace and are searching in vain for fulfillment. God did not create us just to be born, have the easiest time on earth as possible, and then pass away. The Bible teaches that at the core of every human being is a soul that was made to worship and give glory to God. The Bible also says that God uses ordinary people to lead others to knowledge of Him. As Christians, God gives us the honor of sharing His love and grace with anyone that we meet. In every conversation or question about your child, you have the opportunity to tell people about a perfect God of grace. Beneath the surface of life and what we see just in our own home, God is using all things to draw people to a saving relationship with Him. On top of God working in your life, He may also be linking you to people in the world around you that you may have never met if not for your experience. You have a unique story to point people to Christ. You have the opportunity to tell people about the blessing of your child, and God's grace and comfort through the challenges.

How do I handle pity?

Enter through the narrow gate. For wide is the gate and broad is the road that leads to destruction, and many enter through it. But small is the gate and narrow the road that leads to life, and only a few find it.

MATTHEW 7:13-14 NIV

For what does it profit a man to gain the whole world, and forfeit his soul?

MARK 8:36 NASB

Inevitably, Shepherd will continue to receive looks of pity. As his proud mother I know that there is really nothing to pity him for. He has a more than fortunate life - a remarkable father, a loving environment, and a safe home in a country of freedom. While I appreciate the instinctual compassion people feel for his unforeseen challenges, I believe that it is important for parents of different children to keep pity in perspective to find the proper place it belongs.

We live in a world that the Bible says has been broken since the first contamination of sin. Ever still, the world is growing colder, angrier, and increasingly obscene. The Bible teaches in Matthew 7:13-14 that there are two paths in life: a wide gate and broad road that lead to destruction, and a small gate and narrow road that lead to life. Regardless of appearance, social status, or IQ level, many people in this world are walking along the broad road that leads to destruction and ends in an eternity without Christ. According to Jesus, that is the condition to be pitied above all else.

What is your foremost prayer for your child? Is it for happiness, fame, or wealth? Is it for comfort or a "normal" life? My honest answer is that before and above anything, I pray that Shepherd will "enter through the narrow gate". I pray that he will be one of what the Bible calls the few who find it. What would it matter if Shepherd had two hands with which he built empires, but at the end of life lost his soul? Do you feel sorry for yourself or your child? We must all evaluate whether or not we are placing greater importance on present circumstances or on eternity. The proper place for pity is not on your child, it is on a world where normal is the wide gate and broad road.

IS THE BIBLE A CRUTCH TO MAKE WEAK PEOPLE FEEL BETTER ABOUT THEIR LIVES?

You, however, continue in the things you have learned and become convinced of, knowing from whom you have learned them

2 TIMOTHY 3:14 NASB

For momentary, light affliction is producing for us an eternal weight of glory far beyond all comparison, while we look not at the things which are seen, but at the things which are not seen; for the things which are seen are temporal, but the things which are not seen are eternal.

2 CORINTHIANS 4:17-18 NASB

People may wonder if applying the Bible to your situation is just to make you feel better about your life since you cannot change it anyway. You might be wondering that yourself. I believe that you *can* change your situation - you can choose to believe or not believe the Bible, and that choice actually changes everything. The life of a parent who believes that their child is unique by God's design is very different from the life of a parent who believes that their child is unique by chance. In ministry, my husband and I have witnessed many individuals and families encounter life-changing circumstances, with each choosing to either turn towards God or against God. Every person either did one or the other, and it was each one's decision to make. Choosing to respond in faith during any situation is not easy, let alone one in which you find yourself suddenly standing out among the crowds. Having a faithful response may even be hard for the crowds themselves to imagine. "Oh I'm sure that probably makes you feel a little better." "I suppose that's a nicer way of looking at things". "Ah yes, it's good to put a positive spin on your situation". "I guess since there are no other answers or solutions it's better to just have faith that God has a plan." Patronizing or insincere remarks may come along but God tells us to "continue in the things you have learned and become convinced of" and to "look not at the things which are seen, but the things which are unseen… which are eternal".

God tells us "In all circumstances take up the shield of faith, with which you can extinguish all the flaming darts of the evil one;" (Ephesians 6:16 ESV), and promises that "every word of God proves true; He is a shield to those who take refuge in him." (Proverbs 30:5 ESV). If someone suggests that your faith is a crutch, we actually see from these verses in Ephesians and Proverbs that technically, that opinion is biblically inaccurate because your faith is described in Scripture as your shield. Yet I suppose that if a crutch is meant in the purest sense as something to be leaned on, then wouldn't the entire point of having faith be to lean on it?

The Bible describes faith like a piece of spiritual armor. We lean on the promises of God not as a crutch just to feel better, but because of the belief that His words are true even when facing life's greatest hurdles. This book is not about turning lemons into lemonade. My son is not a lemon, and neither is your child. You must resolutely choose how you will view your family life. I choose to believe what the Bible says about children, and I pray you do also.

ONCE I MOVE ON, WILL DISCOURAGING MOMENTS STILL OCCASIONALLY COME IN THE FUTURE?

Do not be anxious about anything, but in everything by prayer and supplication with thanksgiving let your requests be made known to God. And the peace of God, which surpasses all understanding, will guard your hearts and your minds in Christ Jesus.

PHILIPPIANS 4:6-7 ESV

Personally I call these "stinger moments". For example, a brief little sting in my heart when I imagine the moment Shepherd walks alone into a new classroom. I've had a few stinger moments as I've watched Shep play happily and thought to myself, "Wow, I wish I could freeze this moment where he is totally clueless that he's different and he doesn't even know how to be embarrassed by the people staring at him right now. I wish he could stay blissfully unaware for as long as possible." However I know that day will eventually come - the day he overhears a whisper or a snicker, and he realizes it is about him.

Your heart may occasionally be apprehensive about future social situations or how your child will react once aware of his difference. Instead of turning to anxiety, God invites us to bring absolutely all concerns to Him. Pray continuously for your child, for yourself as a parent, and for his influencers such as friends, teachers, coaches, and physicians. The Bible promises, "the peace of God, which surpasses all understanding, will guard your hearts and your minds in Christ Jesus."

I would like to give a friendly caution to beware of comparisons. As unbecoming as it is for an average person passing you on the street to feel more fortunate about their circumstances in relation to yours, it is just as unflattering for me to look at another family and think, "Well I'm lucky because it could always be worse and I'm thankful I'm not in their shoes." You may wonder how others deal with their challenges, and people may wonder the same thing about you. Yet in talking with other special needs parents, they all respond that God's grace has miraculously been proportional to their life's demands. Be patient with those around you who express that they cannot fathom your strength and again give glory to the God who has given you the ability. We tend to view life through the lens of relativity, constantly comparing our lives to others and judging it as better or worse than someone else. Yet the challenges, just like the blessings, in our life are designed *for us.* Your struggle is not greater or smaller, it is just yours, and theirs is just theirs.

IS INTERVENTION VALUABLE?

Without counsel plans fail, but with many advisers they succeed.
PROVERBS 15:22 ESV

Intervention can include medical screenings and exams, specialist evaluations, therapy (physical, occupational, speech, cognitive, social, behavioral, etc), biomechanical devices, adaptive equipment, special educational programs, or counseling. While these can be valuable resources to support or enrich the development of your child, the necessity or importance of intervention can only be determined based on your family's needs and individual situation. It is your choice when and how much intervention enters your life.

Personally, my husband and I have taken advantage of as much information and as many resources as are available. During the latter stage of pregnancy, we saw an obstetrical specialist to track Shepherd's growth and development and it gave us great insight into what to expect. We knew by the time he was born that both arms were going to be the same length and that there would possibly be some slight mobility at the end of his left arm where a wrist is typically located. After Shepherd's birth, our pediatrician referred us to a geneticist, cardiologist, orthopedist, and occupational therapist who all confirmed that he did not have any underlying conditions related to his limb difference. The occupational therapy has been extremely helpful in teaching Shepherd how to best adapt his growing body to a world that is built for people with two hands. Do children naturally adapt? Sure, but as a new mom I had no clue how to ideally teach my child to make the most of his form or to strategically handle tasks. I appreciate the years of experience that his therapists have brought into our home. At some point we will have to decide if Shepherd would benefit from the use of a prosthetic hand for certain activities, but as a toddler, he is developing wonderfully without one.

The opportunities out there for helpful intervention vary. Some programs or networks are well known, whereas others may require research to find. Some may benefit your child more or less than others. As technology continues to advance in the area of diagnostic tests, therapies, and medical equipment, our family's approach is to pray for the Lord's direction and to keep an open mind to any possible solutions as needs arise.

HOW CAN ADOPTED CHILDREN AND THEIR PARENTS DEAL WITH FEELING DIFFERENT?

Religion that God our Father accepts as pure and faultless is this: to look after orphans and widows in their distress and to keep oneself from being polluted by the world.

JAMES 1:27 NIV

In the same way we also, when we were children, were enslaved to the elementary principles of the world. But when the fullness of time had come, God sent forth His Son, born of woman, born under the law, to redeem those who were under the law, so that we might receive adoption as sons. And because you are sons, God has sent the Spirit of His Son into our hearts, crying, "Abba! Father!" So you are no longer a slave, but a son, and if a son, then an heir through God.

GALATIANS 4:3-8 ESV

The first and only biological relative that I have ever known to date is actually Shepherd. I was adopted as a newborn in

South Korea by my American father and Korean mother. My parents met while my dad was stationed with the US Air Force in Unijeonbu, and a year after their marriage, they found me on their doorstep! From that day, I had a family that included grandparents, aunts, uncles, and dozens of cousins in Korea, Florida, Georgia, and Louisiana! Josh and I are currently awaiting the finalization of the arduous but worthwhile process of international adoption to bring home a daughter and a son. When we finally return from Democratic Republic of Congo, they will be Anna Rose and Abraham Reavis, and we are praying that day arrives soon! Josh also has two cousins that are adopted from within the United States. We are passionate supporters of adoption and understand the mixed reactions these special children and their parents sometimes face. While adoption is making a child one's own, the adopted children frequently stand out and it is not always easy for them to feel completely accepted by society as indeed a member of their own family. I say "by society" because within my family, I was totally accepted. Most of my family called me Sarah, partly because it was easier to pronounce than my birth name Seana, and partly because it made me feel very all-American indeed! I never heard the term "adopted daughter", "adopted niece", or talk of biological versus non-biological. In fact, my family was so receiving of me that when my father told me at the age of eight that I was adopted, I was shocked. Even with all of my blonde-haired and blue-eyed cousins around me, I still never caught on that I wasn't blood related to a single one of them!

Outside of my family was a different story. While today there is a lot more diversity within families and society, growing up I was the only person that I knew of who was adopted. There were stares from strangers at my dad and I. When I was with both parents, it was usually assumed that I "belonged" to my mom but my dad must have been a stepparent. Classmates asked continually if I wished I were with my "real" mom and dad, or if I knew where they were. People even asked me if my parents adopted me because they could not have kids "of their own", as if I had to of been Plan B. Even today adoptive parents can expect at least a few differences from building their family biologically. A pregnancy is regularly met with congratulations, whereas occasionally the news of adoption brings many questions about cost, medical issues, or if there is the possibility of "ruining" your "real" family by bringing in someone from the outside. My friend Renee Swanda is a mother to thirteen children, some biological and some adopted from Ethiopia, Ghana, and China. She recommends that adoptive parents keep in mind that usually the voices of uncertainty come from genuine hearts of concern that the parents will be hurt.

Adoptive children may also hear strangers ask of their parents questions such as, "Which kids are yours and which are adopted?" or "Which of the siblings are 'really related'". Differences attract attention but as with any other visible difference, the attention is usually simply curiosity or at least well intentioned. Renee and her husband have taught their children that seldom does anyone outside the "adoption world" aim to make an adopted child feel discounted. They also emphasize the importance of graciously responding to every question or comment with respect, understanding that a parent or child of adoption is usually more sensitive to the terminology that seems to be underlining their difference. I appreciate that my family always emphasized to me that no one meant for their comments to be upsetting and they gave reassurance that I was in fact "theirs" and that we were "really related" because they were my parents, period. We will continually teach Anna Rose, Abraham, and Shepherd that they are in fact, "real" siblings and no one is more brother or sister than the other. They are our own, and we will be raising them all equally, in the same home with the same values, food, and resources.

In James 1:27, God instructs Christians to care for orphans. In other biblical translations you may see the verse written as "visit orphans". The verse does not mean that every couple is called to adopt children, but it does show us how important orphans are to God and how much He cares for children in need. If you are a Christian, Galatians 4:3-8 proclaims that *you* have actually been adopted by God the Father because of your faith in Jesus Christ. When we are lost without Christ, we are slaves of this world, slaves of self and sin. However, verse 7 tells us that when we place our faith in Jesus as Savior, "you are no longer a slave... but an heir through God." The wonderful thing about paying the cost for the adoption of children on earth is the illustration it is of our own adoption by our Heavenly Father, who paid the price of His only begotten son Jesus, "to redeem those who were under the law" (v. 5).

I hope that our experience will encourage families who may stand out because they have been brought together through adoption. Becoming a parent by birth or by adoption are both beautiful miracles that show how much our God loves to create families and bring them together!

"It has been our goal to provide our children with a Biblical worldview of adoption. Many times the world has portrayed the idea of adoption in a negative light. God views adoption so differently. It is the picture God uses for the wondrous miracle of salvation... Each of our adoptions has their own unique stories. The cord that runs through them all though is that we felt called to adopt and God gave us the desire to parent another child. He set us on the path (Proverbs 3:5-6) and put the desire in our heart and we delighted in it (Psalm 37:4)".

-Renee Swanda.

DOES THE BIBLE SAY, "BLESSED ARE THE DIFFERENT"?

There is no verse that reads, "Blessed are the Different". At the same time, no verse exists that reads, "Blessed are those with the typical physical body" or "Blessed are those who have all the desirable traits". Jesus and the world often differ on what they consider to be blessed and why. The Sermon on the Mount offers an intriguing list of Jesus' qualifications:

> *And he opened his mouth and taught them, saying:*
>
> *"Blessed are the poor in spirit, for theirs is the kingdom of heaven.*
>
> *Blessed are those who mourn, for they shall be comforted.*
>
> *Blessed are the meek, for they shall inherit the earth.*
>
> *Blessed are those who hunger and thirst for righteousness, for they shall be satisfied.*
>
> *Blessed are the merciful, for they shall receive mercy.*
>
> *Blessed are the pure in heart, for they shall see God.*

> *Blessed are the peacemakers, for they shall be called sons of God.*
>
> *Blessed are those who are persecuted for righteousness' sake, for theirs is the kingdom of heaven.*
>
> *Blessed are you when others revile you and persecute you and utter all kinds of evil against you falsely on my account. Rejoice and be glad, for your reward is great in heaven, for so they persecuted the prophets who were before you."*

MATTHEW 5:2-12, ESV

You are far more likely to hear parents complimented for their child's vocal talents or pageant awards than their child's humility or purity. You are also more likely to hear parents themselves express that they are blessed because their child is accomplished in sports or gifted academically. While talents, skills, and natural beauty are all blessings of God, it is important to note the specific characteristics that Jesus himself deemed worthy to be listed as blessed. I truly want Shepherd to be blessed so I had to ask myself, "Which do I prefer: for him to have one hand and be merciful, righteous, peaceful, and humble, or have two hands and have none or few of the qualities that Jesus said are truly valuable?" You may be wondering why it cannot be both, why I would not ardently prefer that Shepherd have both hands *and* a blamelessly pure heart. Still, remember that Jesus' list made no mention of any physical or mental features, so they are obviously not God's determining factors for living a blessed life. If my son is merciful, Jesus calls him blessed, regardless of how he looks compared to others. If your child is pure in heart, Jesus calls your priceless child blessed, regardless of his or her difference. A physical body does not necessarily amplify nor diminish the possibility to be blessed.

It is my honest desire that the Scripture passages that were reviewed in this book are an encouragement to you as they have been to me. As I think back to the moment my husband and I sat in the sonogram room and were told that our child was different, I wish I could relive that day and the weeks that followed. I wish I had reacted according to the joy I feel now. Rather than having a similar regret, I hope that you continue to draw confidence from God's Word as your family grows. I am thankful that while yesterday is gone, God has given us today! May you always believe that the life of your child is a gift, and that "every good and perfect gift is from above". (James 1:17 NIV)

Acknowledgments

I would like to express my sincere gratitude to all those who have supported the production of this book. Thank you for the sacrificial time and effort taken to contribute testimonies, proof, edit, and spread the word about this project. I will never take for granted that the publication of this book is due to the generous donations of family and friends. Your desire to partner and invest in this ministry to families is genuinely appreciated!

About the Author

Seana Reavis lives in Jacksonville, FL with her husband Josh. They have one son named Shepherd and are in the process of adopting two children from the Democratic Republic of Congo. As a pastor's wife and mother of a child with special needs she has a passion to communicate the hope of Christ to other families who may struggle with the realities of raising a special needs child.